It's Too Loud

by Linda Lott
illustrated by Karen Lee

 HOUGHTON MIFFLIN   BOSTON

I hear a loud bark
in my room.

I hear a loud car
in the street.

I hear a loud crash
in the lunch room.

I hear a loud drum
in the parade.

I hear a loud truck
in the street.

I hear loud music
in my house.

It is not loud now!